TAMPA

A MANY SPLENDORED CITY

"TAMPA" is a co-publication of The Tampa Tribune and Surfside Publishing, Tampa, Florida.

ISBN 0-942084-44-6
Library of Congress # 90-071579
Printed in the United States of America

Requests for discounts on large quantities should be addressed to:
The Tampa Tribune
202 S. Parker Street
Tampa, FL 33606
Attention: Dom Cassano

MANAGER SPECIAL PROJECTS
Dom Cassano

EDITOR
Carol Dyches

DESIGNER
Ann R. Griffin

CREATIVE COORDINATORS
Tim Lancaster
Joyce Lessard

COVER PHOTO
Skip Gandy

PHOTOGRAPHY / TRIBUNE PROMOTION
Connie Brown
Matt Larson

PHOTOGRAPHY COORDINATOR
Joan Wessinger

PHOTOGRAPHY / TRIBUNE NEWS
Robert Burke, Todd Chappel, John Coffeen, Jay Conner, Chuck Ferlita, Fred Fox, Dave Geiger, Barry Katz, Cliff McBride, Candace Mundy, Skip O'Rourke, Jim Reed, Gary Rings, Al Satterwhite, Jim Tuten, Beth Wilson

CONTRIBUTING PHOTOGRAPHERS
George Cott/Chroma, Inc., Gwen Hughes, Becky Sexton Larson, A.C. McCarthy, Selbypic, Christopher Wright

SPECIAL THANKS
Tony Noriega, Production Group Associates, Photography

PRODUCTION STAFF
Thomas Arduengo
Harry Kuligofski
Cliff Minier

Keith Bezanson
William Clark
David Dean
Kevin Foley
Terrence Griffiths
Monte Hamel
Mary Kroepel
Kathleen Stolle

EXECUTIVE OFFICES

SANDRA W. FREEDMAN
MAYOR

Welcome to Tampa!

Even if you're a native, "welcome" seems an appropriate introduction to this portrait of Tampa. It may hold almost as many discoveries for you as it does for first-time visitors and out-of-state readers.

I hope this book gives you some sense of who we are. In a way, Tampa's 1990 All America City award sums it all up. We earned that honor through communitywide efforts to tackle challenges and make this a better place for every resident.

Even this publication is a product of community effort. Countless public and private citizens and organizations provided information, photographs and assistance. I am very grateful to everyone who participated and especially to The Tampa Tribune for putting it all in print.

Enjoy your tour.

Best wishes,

Sandra W. Freedman

Sandra W. Freedman
Mayor

The Tampa Tribune gratefully acknowledges all those who contributed to the publication of this book. A community effort, it is a shining example of Tampa's spirit.

ACKNOWLEDGEMENTS

City of Tampa, Office of the Mayor
Tampa Hillsborough Convention and Visitors Association
Ybor City Chamber of Commerce
Hillsborough County School System
MacDill Air Force Base, Tampa Port Authority
Tampa International Airport, Peter O. Knight Airport

Hampton Dunn

Arts Council of Hillsborough County
Henry B. Plant Museum, Tampa Museum of Art
The Tampa Ballet, The Florida Orchestra
The Tampa Theatre
Museum of Science & Industry
Children's Museum

Hillsborough Area Regional Transit

Busch Gardens/Adventure Island
Lowry Park Zoological Garden

Tampa Bay Buccaneers, Tampa Bay Rowdies, Cincinnati Reds
Michelob/American Invitational–Stadium Jumping, Inc.
Hall of Fame Bowl Committee
Tampa Greyhound Track, Tampa Bay Downs, Tampa JaiAlai

Special Olympics

Alfred Austin Development Corp., Opus South Corporation, Paragon Group
The Wilson Company, Trammel Crow Company

Beulah Baptist Church, Palma Ceia Methodist Church, Palma Ceia Presbyterian Church
Rodeph Sholom Synagogue, Sacred Heart Church

Academy of the Holy Names, Gorrie Elementary School, Hillel School of Tampa
Hillsborough Community College, Hillsborough High School, Jesuit High School, Lockhart Elementary School
Plant High School, Tampa Preparatory School, University of South Florida, University of Tampa

Boy Scouts of America, Suncoast Girl Scout Council Inc., YMCA

Tampa/Hillsborough County Public Library

Old Hyde Park Village, Tampa Bay Center, University Square Mall, West Shore Plaza, Ybor Square

H. Lee Moffitt Cancer Center and Research Institute
Shriners Hospital for Crippled Children, St. Joseph's Hospital, The Tampa General Hospital

Armani's Restaurant, Bayshore Conch Club, Bern's Steak House, Cactus Club, Cafe Creole, Colonnade Restaurant
Columbia Restaurant, Ho Ho Chinois, Oystercatchers, Villanova Restaurant, Wright's Gourmet

Smith & Associates, Realtors

Great American Corporation

Hicks Advertising Group, Roberts & Hice Inc. Public Relations
Russell, Alexander, Frederick & Co., The Bank of Tampa

The Festival of Trees

Courtesy of Tampa Museum of Art:
Page 55. Installation photograph of *Icons of Postwar Art: Painting and Sculpture from the Braman Collection*, 1985.
C. Paul Jennewein (American, 1890-1978), *Over the Waves*, 1927, bronze, h. 54 in., Bequest of the artist, 1983.
Red-Figure Calyx Krater, Attic, c. 440. B.C., Attributed to the Menelaos Painter, h. 14 1/2 in

TAMPA

TAMPA

Like many of Florida's major population centers, Tampa is far younger than history might have decreed.

Spanish explorers investigated this part of the Gulf coast nearly five centuries ago, and England held title briefly during the 18th century, leaving a legacy in such names as the Hillsborough River.

Still, the community began taking permanent shape only in 1824, when Fort Brooke was established at the mouth of the river in present-day downtown Tampa. Soon the area was populated by a lively mix of Cubans, Germans, Irish, Italians, Scots, Spaniards and native Southerners attracted to the opportunities on this new frontier.

A world of reasons to shine

That early fusion of cultures is reflected in today's Tampa: a blend of yankee ingenuity and southern hospitality, expressed with an international accent.

Pressed to characterize the city, some point to its standing as a nationally-respected business center, while others emphasize the countless attractions of a top vacation destination. Still others say simply that Tampa is a great place to live.

This is a community inventive enough to turn the Gasparilla pirate invasion into one of America's most festive events. It's big enough to host the Volvo World Cup International showjumping finals and two NFL Super Bowls . . . and resourceful enough to be recognized as an All America City.

Local residents relish their bragging rights to the origins of scheduled commercial air service, the world's longest continuous sidewalk, the nation's best airport, Florida's top cargo port and a unique Latin quarter.

Tampa is a kaleidoscope of impressions: silver minarets crowning a fanciful 19th century building, African animals roaming a theme park veldt, a Spanish restaurant's handpainted tiles, office buildings standing by a sheltered bay, a stadium filled with football fans and, perhaps most of all, people whose extraordinary geniality is absolutely genuine.

Downtown Tampa, from Bayshore Boulevard

The Davis Islands
bridges, with the
Bayshore beyond,
and a shrimp
boat idling on
Tampa Bay

Symbols of two
centuries: the
Harbour Island
planned
community and a
University of
Tampa minaret

Handpainted tiles
and 7th Avenue in
Ybor City, Tampa's
own Latin quarter

Crowd pleasers:
the Gasparilla
celebration and NFL
football at Tampa
Stadium

The Tampa Bay
Performing Arts
Center and a hotel
in the Westshore
business district

F-16's at MacDill Air
Force Base, high
technology at the
University of South
Florida and the
state's #1 port

Events of the late 19th century changed Tampa's fortunes forever.

Connecticut native Henry Bradley Plant brought the railroad here in 1884 and then capped his achievement with the Tampa Bay Hotel, a 511-room fantasy that remains the city's most distinctive landmark.

At about the same time, the Tampa Board of Trade encouraged prominent cigar manufacturers to relocate their factories from Key West. Thus began the industry that would earn Tampa the title of "Cigar City."

A vibrant and A varied economy

More than symbols of transportation, travel accommodations and industry, these progress points represent a partnership between entrepreneurial newcomers and established local business leaders that continues to drive Tampa's broadbased economy.

The business and financial capital of Florida's largest standard metropolitan area, this market has earned high marks from the nation's corporate leaders as a location for new or expanded facilities.

Transportation has long played a major role. A 1914 flight across Tampa Bay was the first in scheduled commercial aviation history. Tampa International Airport has been consistently voted best in the nation, and the Port of Tampa is Florida's top cargo-handling port, as well as an emerging pleasure cruise center.

The hotels are still first rate, and the Tampa Convention Center on the downtown waterfront gives visitors a splendid new place to congregate.

Fine cigars remain a source of local pride, although they do not dominate Tampa industry as they once did. No single product could in an economy that runs the gamut from seafood and sportswear to shipbuilding and steel and from family owned businesses to regional and headquarters offices of major U.S. corporations.

Medicine covers a equally wide spectrum, from product research and development to comprehensive general hospitals, a regional cancer research and treatment center, a VA hospital, three heart centers and a Shriners hospital for crippled children.

Generations after the founding of Fort Brooke, Tampa's original industry, the military, is a substantial force in the business community. MacDill Air Force Base is a strategic U.S. defense post and a vital trade center for central Florida's huge retired military population.

City Hall, reflected in a modern office tower

Scenes from the
cityscape: the
Esplanade, a
skybridge and
an elevated
people mover

The Barnett Plaza
and NCNB Plaza
office towers,
overlooking
Plant Park

Riding the
Hillsborough River
through downtown
and taking a break
on the Franklin
Street Mall

The new Tampa Convention Center, the One Tampa City Center and One Harbour Place office buildings and the Hyatt Regency Hotel

Tackling projects large and small, from a U.S. Navy refueling ship to advanced technology

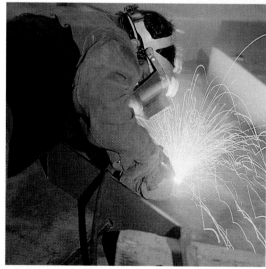

Ybor City, where a historic factory houses offices and shops and workers still make cigars by hand

Working near the water: Bayport Plaza on Tampa Bay (right) and Bayshore Place on Bayshore Boulevard

In Westshore, Florida's second-largest office district: 4200 Cypress (above and far left) and Austin Center South

Working in
Westshore:
Paragon Center
(right), the
Sheraton Grand
Hotel (below) and
Westshore Center

Tampa International
Airport (above),
Peter O. Knight
executive airport and
the Tampa Airport
Marriott Hotel

Ships for work and play at the Port of Tampa, 7th-largest in the U.S.

An F-16 at MacDill,
a replica of the
plane that flew the
first scheduled
commercial flight
and shrimp boats
in port east of
downtown

The H. Lee Moffitt
Cancer Center and
Research Institute
(right) and
St. Joseph's Hospital

The Tampa General
Hospital (above), the
Shriners Hospital for
Crippled Children
(far left) and a medical
office tower at
Tampa General

Just across the river from downtown Tampa's soaring office towers stands a modest schoolhouse, restored from a structure built in 1850 to educate a pioneer settler's daughter and his neighbors' children.

The First Baptist Church, originally chartered in 1859, occupies a corner nearby, and the First Methodist Church, whose founding dates to 1851, is located not far away, at the north end of downtown.

These structures represent two of the strongest threads in the fabric of local community life.

The countywide public school system, which is the 12th largest in the U.S., is

Bright minds and deep convictions

augmented by more than 110 private and parochial schools, and the curriculum responds to a broad diversity of interests, from college preparatory studies and vocational training to education for students with special needs.

Higher education offers an almost unlimited array of possibilities, from two-year associate programs to post-graduate and professional degrees.

The University of Tampa, a private, four-year institution, has made its home in the former Tampa Bay Hotel on the downtown riverfront since 1933.

The University of South Florida first welcomed students to its north Tampa campus in 1960 and now ranks as the state's second-largest public university.

Hillsborough Community College, a member of the state community college system, has campuses throughout the county, and private, post-secondary schools offer career-oriented degrees, as well as academic studies.

The public library system is a learning institution in its own right, offering a bookmobile, books-by-mail, Talking Books, children's programs and adult literacy tutoring, as well as more than 1.1 million books, a wide selection of audio-visual materials and an important collection of historic Florida photographs.

Religion reflects the abiding tenets of a multicultural population, from the Protestant and Catholic churches founded by Tampa's pioneer congregations to synagogues, temples and houses of worship devoted to virtually every western and eastern faith.

Sacred Heart Church, downtown Tampa

The University of
South Florida: the
engineering building,
a high tech
experiment and an
archeological dig

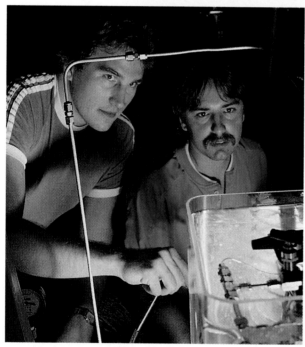

TAMPA BAY HOTEL

Henry B. Plant built this ornate Moorish structure at a cost of $3 million. Opened in 1891, it became the social and cultural center of early Tampa. During the Spanish American War it was headquarters for troops going to Cuba and housed such visitors as Col. Theodore Roosevelt, Clara Barton, Richard Harding Davis and Gen. Nelson Miles. Purchased by the City of Tampa in 1905, it has served as the main building of the Univ. of Tampa since 1933.

FLORIDA BOARD OF STATE AND HISTORIC MEMORIALS   1961

The University of Tampa's unique main building and Hillsborough Community College's Dale Mabry campus

Hillsborough High
School, Palma Ceia
Presbyterian Church
and a PAL track
and field day at
Hillsborough High

The Palma Ceia
Methodist Church
sanctuary and the
carefully-renovated
Gorrie Elementary
School

A gifted education program for elementary school students and landmarks within the religious community

Plant High School, the Jesuit High School chapel and a Jesuit student assembly

Scenes from
Lockhart School's
international folk
festival and students
at a private
preparatory school

A student rowing crew, the Tampa Preparatory School entrance and Hebrew Academy preschoolers observing Hanukkah

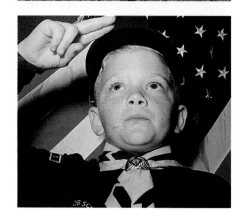

Strong traditions,
from the Academy
of the Holy Names
to Girl Scout
recycling efforts and
Cub Scout salutes

Rodeph Sholom synagogue, an early settlers' schoolhouse and Beulah Baptist Church's Reverend Leon Lowry

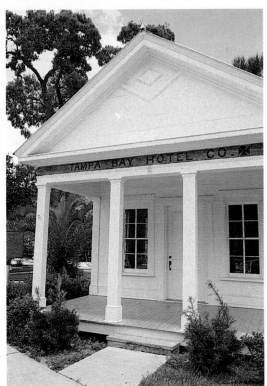

In Tampa, the arts aren't confined to museums and concert halls. They spill over into the streets, sidewalks and parks, even into office buildings and retail centers.

There *are* museums and concert halls, of course. The Tampa Museum of Art offers changing exhibits, as well as a permanent collection of Greek and southern Italian antiquities, and the University of South Florida Art Museum showcases contemporary work by major American and European artists.

Two museums are devoted to local history: the Henry B. Plant Museum, which preserves the Tampa Bay Hotel's splendor; and the Ybor City State

A showcase for many talents

Museum, a view of the Latin quarter that made this the world's cigar capital.

Those who prefer more active "hands-on" encounters find a wealth of experiences at the Children's Museum of Tampa and the Museum of Science and Industry.

The Tampa Theatre, a restored 1926 movie palace, is a treat for both the eyes and ears.

Every year, hundreds of artists (and hundreds of thousands of art patrons) convene at the Gasparilla Sidewalk Art Festival. And almost any open space – from a retail center courtyard to a public park – is likely to be filled with arts and crafts any time of year.

Even a routine business day walk through downtown Tampa can be festive. Chamber musicians may be performing in an office building lobby. Outside, a tree-shaded plaza may resound with reggae rhythms. On the Franklin Street Mall, the lunch hour crowd might include mimes, jugglers or puppeteers.

While local and touring entertainers perform in a wide variety of venues, from the University of South Florida Sun Dome to an Ybor City theatre, the undisputed focal point is the Tampa Bay Performing Arts Center.

Unequaled by any other such facility in the south, the downtown Tampa center is comprised of three theatres, where performances range from local symphony orchestra concerts, ballet and community theatre presentations to touring productions of one-man shows and Broadway musicals.

The Tampa Theatre, restored to its 1926 splendor

The Tampa Bay Performing Arts Center, where events include classic ballet and African folk dance

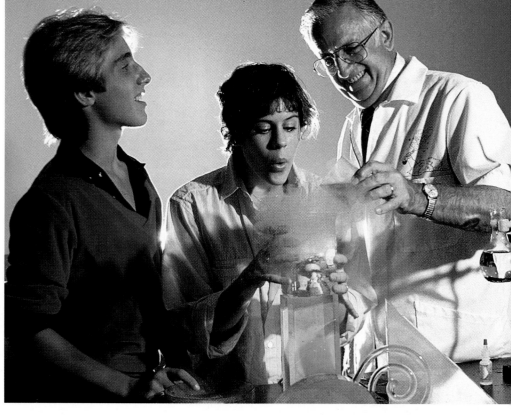

Hands-on experiences at the Museum of Science and Industry (above left and right) and the Children's Museum of Tampa

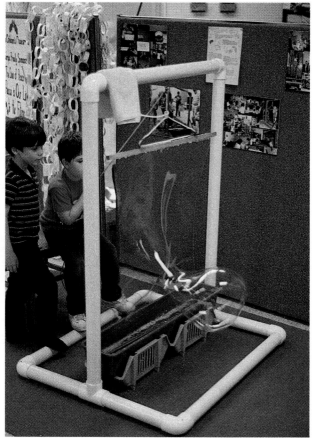

The Florida Orchestra,
whose concerts range
from the classics to
pops, and the historic
Henry B. Plant
Museum

Bits n Pieces puppets
and the much-
photographed Red
Couch, in
town for a
Tampa Museum
of Art exhibition

A Tampa Museum
of Art gallery and
representative pieces
from the Museum's
permanent collections

An outdoor mural in
Ybor City and
examples of public
art in and near
downtown

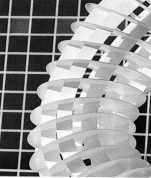

The Gasparilla
Sidewalk Art Festival
(above), the colorful
India Festival and
one of many arts
and crafts shows

Fascinating rhythms
at Busch Gardens
(right), the
Performing Arts
Center and
downtown's
public spaces

It's easy to understand why this area ranks among the top ten all-around U.S. vacation destinations. Tampa has a natural affinity for fun.

Consider three events as evidence.

In winter, the city and thousands of visitors celebrate Tampa's "capture" by pirates. The only festival in the world dedicated to such a theme, Gasparilla originated in 1904 and has grown into a non-stop round of parades and parties.

Tampa is also home to the Florida State Fair, held at a site just east of the city. And in the fall, bizarre becomes the norm, when outrageously costumed revelers gather in Ybor City for Guavaween, Tampa's own version of Halloween.

Top college football teams meet annually in the Hall of Fame Bowl. Almost before the cheers have faded, Tampa welcomes a who's who of other competitors: the GTE Suncoast Seniors Classic's PGA Tour stars, the Gasparilla Distance Classic's world class runners, the President's Cup Regatta's university rowing crews and the Michelob American Invitational's equestrian elite.

For some fans, parimutuel wagering is the name of the game. In Tampa, you can always bet on fun, from greyhound and thoroughbred racing to jai-alai, which turns a seemingly simple task – catching and hurling a ball (or *pelota*) with a basket (or *cesta*) – into the world's fastest game.

Celebrating every season

"Wild behavior" of a different kind lasts year-round at the Lowry Park Zoo and at Busch Gardens, a 300-acre African theme park with the nation's fourth largest zoo.

Sports fans welcome every season. In addition to the NFL's Tampa Bay Buccaneers and pro soccer's Tampa Bay Rowdies, there are championship calibre college baseball teams, AAU track and field competition, Nissan World Challenge auto racing and the Cincinnati Reds, who train each spring in nearby Plant City.

Even on a calendar where special attractions are almost routine, some events are so extraordinary as to warrant worldwide attention.

In 1989, Tampa became only the second city in the United States ever selected for the prestigious Volvo World Cup Finals, the equestrian world's premier showjumping event. Five years earlier, Tampa hosted Super Bowl XVIII so successfully that the National Football League chose to return for the Silver Anniversary Super Bowl in 1991.

A festive moment
at Tampa Stadium

Gasparilla
pirates, staging
their capture
of the city

The Florida State
Fair midway and a
parade of
Guavaween
celebrants

Year-round
competition: the
Tampa Bay
Buccaneers, the
Hall of Fame Bowl,
the Cincinnati Reds
in spring training and
the Tampa Bay
Rowdies

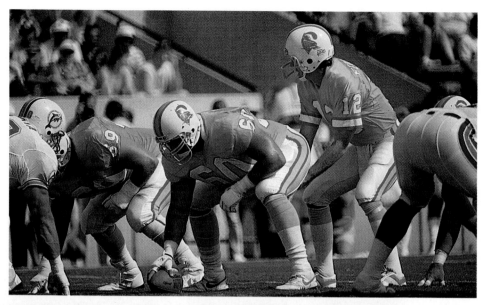

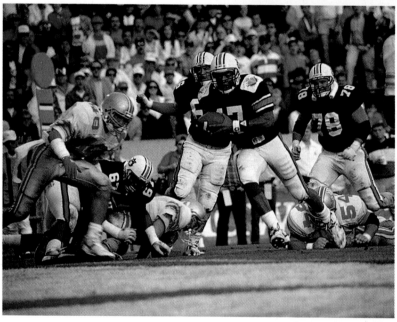

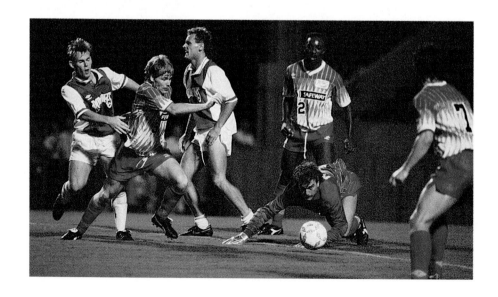

Tampa Stadium, filled with football fans and with showjumping gates for the annual Michelob American Invitational

Fun you can bet on,
at Tampa Jai Alai,
Tampa Bay Downs
and the Tampa
Greyhound Track

Great team efforts,
from the polo field
to the college
basketball courts

Right on course: the
GTE Suncoast
Seniors Classic (right)
and the Gasparilla
Distance Classic

Winter rowing practice
in the Florida sun and
the natural wonders of
the Lowry Park Zoo

Busch Gardens,
where attractions
range from
entertainment and a
Moroccan Village
to free-roaming
African animals

Some of the fun at
Adventure Island and
community support
for the annual
Festival of Trees,
which benefits
abused children

TAMPA

The picture postcard image of Florida is indelibly printed in the mind: golf, beaches and radiant sunshine.

That's a fair introduction to the good times in Tampa. But local residents will tell you there's much more to what is popularly called the "quality of life."

There is golf, of course; public and private courses are open year-round. There are also scores of public tennis courts, 85 baseball diamonds and nearly 200 public parks, picnic areas and playgrounds.

In a city ringed by marinas and backyard docks, there are almost too many water sports to mention, but even a cursory list would have to include

A year-round place in the sun

fresh and salt water fishing, water skiing, power boating and virtually every form of sailing. And sun worshippers regularly fill the public beach on Tampa Bay.

Local Little League and softball teams have collected an impressive number of national championships (*and* sent a number of their players on to major league fame).

There's an equally strong emphasis on victory for competitors whose successes are just as meaningful, though they may never make headlines. With the help of enthusiastic volunteers, Tampa annually hosts statewide Special Olympics competition. For that matter, every sunny Saturday seems to occasion walks, runs and cycling events to benefit non-profit organizations.

Perhaps no leisure activity symbolizes Tampa's infinite variety better than dining out. Menus read like a pop quiz in foreign languages, from Spanish restaurants' *arroz con pollo* (yellow rice and chicken) and Greek *baklava* (a pastry layered with honey and almonds) right on through authentic Creole, French, Italian, Mexican and Oriental specialties.

Few newcomers are prepared for the wide selection of fresh seafood or for the discovery of a nationally-rated steak house, with the world's largest wine list.

Even serious shopping is fun. Tampa retailers offer an appealing potpourri of regional malls, upscale boutiques, off-price values and one-of-a-kind originals.

All the colors of a waterborne rainbow

The pleasures of
boating in the city
by the bay

Bay and gulf beaches, just minutes from home

The year-round
call of the great
outdoors

Special moments for
Special Olympians
and a hometown
Little League team

Dining diversity:
Armani's antipasto,
Cactus Club's patio
and Oystercatchers'
seafood restaurant

Bayshore bright spots:
Bayshore Conch Club
and its island-style
specialties (above)
and The Colonnade

Local flavor: Bern's
Steak House (top
left and right),
Cafe Creole and a
platter of Wright's
award-winning
Cuban sandwiches

International accents:
the Columbia
Restaurant (top),
Villanova's northern
Italian fare and
Ho Ho Chinois

Shopping, socializing
and celebrating at
Harbour Island (top
and above) and
West Shore Plaza

Something for every style, from the Old Hyde Park Village shops to University Square Mall

Shopping in the
air conditioned
sunshine of Tampa
Bay Center

Ybor Square: a cigar factory transformed by shops and street festivals

For all its office towers and express highways, private clubs and public parks, every city is essentially a collection of neighborhoods.

In Tampa, which is far younger than most cities of the East and South, neighborhoods can still be traced to easily identified growth periods.

Ybor City has become a new melding of cultures, from descendants of early cigarmakers to artists occupying wrought iron-trimmed studios.

In Tampa Heights, there's new interest in rehabilitating the late 19th century Queen Anne and carpenter Gothic homes of Tampa's first fine neighborhood.

Reflecting a sense of home

Hyde Park, which was developed at the turn of the century, is an area of carefully restored bungalows and imposing homes bordered by Bayshore Boulevard (site of the world's longest uninterrupted sidewalk).

Many of the city's established neighborhoods were built during Florida's 1920's boom, a period that produced Mediterranean Revival architecture, the first bridge across Tampa Bay and the phenomenon of Davis Islands, created from two small islands and the submerged land between them.

Most of Tampa's current residents live in neighborhoods developed since World War II. And what a variety that represents.

Rambling ranch styles overlook canals and the open bay. Highrise condominiums stand near the stately homes along Bayshore. Single- and multi-family homes are part of a unique urban island community. Orange groves have been transformed into master-planned suburbs, where designs range from patio homes to mini-estates that merge with golf course fairways.

As large and multifaceted as Tampa has become, this city has not outgrown its sense of community. Every spring, thousands of people participate in "Paint Your Heart Out, Tampa," a volunteer effort to improve the homes of elderly, low income residents.

That kind of involvement – clearly demonstrating one person's concern for another's well-being – helped make Tampa a 1990 All America City. It's indicative of the city's spirit. And it may be the strongest statement that can be made on the true meaning of "community."

A Mediterranean
Revival reminder
of the 1920's boom

The traditional charm
and public parks of
South Tampa

Homes on
manicured greens
and winding lanes

An almost endless variety of styles, from single-family homes to condominiums and townhomes

The comforts of home, from master-planned suburbs to an island only a channel's width from downtown

Apartments
overlooking a
preserved shoreline
and homes as
distinctive as
their owners

New homes and old and a "Paint Your Heart Out, Tampa" workday for thousands of volunteers

TAMPA

TAMPA HISTORY IN REVIEW

1513

Ponce de Leon explores Florida's west coast, perhaps including Tampa Bay.

1757

First known map of the Tampa Bay area is drawn.

1885

Cigar industry begins in Tampa.

1887

Tampa gets its first charter and electric lighting.

1914

World's first regularly scheduled commercial air service begins between Tampa and St. Petersburg.

1915

Present City Hall is constructed.

1929

The first all-outdoor, all-talking motion picture, *Hell Harbour*, is filmed in Tampa.

1933

Tampa Junior College becomes the University of Tampa and moves to the former Tampa Bay Hotel.

1960

The University of South Florida opens.

1963

President John F. Kennedy presents his last public address four days before his assassination.

1976

The Tampa Bay Buccaneers play their first National Football League game.

1984

Tampa hosts its first NFL Super Bowl.

1824	1834	1865

1824

Fort Brooke is founded, and the first permanent white settlers arrive.

1834

Hillsborough County is created.

1865

Jules Verne depicts Tampa area as launch site in *From the Earth to the Moon*.

1891

Henry B. Plant's Tampa Bay Hotel opens.

1898

Teddy Roosevelt and his Rough Riders camp in Tampa before sailing for Cuba during the Spanish American War.

1904

Gasparilla celebration begins as a May Day festival.

1922

WDAE, Florida's first radio station, goes on the air.

1924

Gandy Bridge opens to Pinellas County, said to be the longest span in the world at the time.

1925

200,000-gallon water tower is built in Sulphur Springs

1934

Davis Causeway (now Courtney Campbell) opens to Clearwater.

1940

Work begins on MacDill Field (now MacDill Air Force Base).

1959

Busch Gardens opens.

1968

Hillsborough Community College opens.

1970

Tampa Stadium opens.

1971

Tampa International Airport's present terminal opens.

1989

The Volvo World Cup Finals are held in Tampa.

1990

Tampa Convention Center opens.

1991

Tampa hosts the Silver Anniversary Super Bowl.